Rules of the Game
in Social Relationships

Josef Pieper

ST. AUGUSTINE'S PRESS
South Bend, Indiana

Library of Congress Cataloging in Publication Data
Names: Pieper, Josef, 1904-1997, author.
Farrelly, Dan, translator
Title: Rules of the game in social relationships / Josef Pieper;
translated by Dan Farrelly.
Other titles: *Grundformen sozialer Spielregeln*. English
Description: South Bend, Indiana: St. Augustines Press, [2016]
Includes bibliographical references and index.
Identifiers: LCCN 2016012552
ISBN 9781587317408 (hardback)
ISBN 9781587317415 (paperbound)
Subjects: LCSH: Sociology.
BISAC: PHILOSOPHY / General.
Classification: LCC HM590 .P5413 2016
DDC 301--dc23 LC
record available at https://lccn.loc.gov/2016012552

St. Augustine's Press
www.staugustine.net

Rules of the Game
in Social Relationships

Books by Josef Pieper from St. Augustine's Press

Christian Idea of Man

Concept of Sin

Death and Immortality

Don't Worry about Socrates

Enthusiasm and Divine Madness

Exercises in the Elements

Happiness and Contemplation

Not Yet the Twilight

In Tune with the World

A Journey to Point Omega

The Platonic Myths

Scholasticism

The Silence of Goethe

The Silence of St. Thomas

Tradition

Tradition as Challenge

Traditional Truth, Poetry, Sacrament

What Catholics Believe

What Does "Academic" Mean?

Table of Contents

Preface

This book was first published in 1933. It was the work of a 27-year-old Assistant at a sociological research institute and was formulated in the requisite scientific jargon. The spontaneous decision to rewrite it in plain language accessible to everyone came to me suddenly as I was reading a single strange sentence, the naivety of which I would never have expected of its author. The sentence expresses the quintessence of an official speech made in the Paulskirche in Frankfurt at the conferring of the Peace Prize of the German Book Trade on 19 September 1976.[1] The speaker and prize-winner – someone I esteem very highly, above all for his realistic mistrust of any kind of ideology – was Max Frisch. On the theme of "We hope" he spoke about the situation in the world after Hiroshima and about the possibility of peace. Peace, as was being said at the time, could not be achieved either through military or diplomatic strategies; instead – and here followed that sentence with its terrifying oversimplification – peace could only be "achieved through the restructuring of society into a community." With these words a spooky *revenant* – the distinction between "community and society," which had been discussed to death – suddenly came back to me. It was the title of the book by Ferdinand Toennies, published one hundred years

1   Edition Suhrkamp 874, Frankfurt 1976

previously. While it is hardly mentioned anymore in sociological literature, its broad subliminal influence has largely
continued. And from an even earlier period I was reminded,
by this unbelievable sentence, of the youthful, exuberant enthusiasm for an exaggerated affirmation of community; of
course, along with this came the early warning in 1924 in
the polemic aimed at us by Helmut Plessner in his "The limits of community."

Countering the same romantic exaggeration of the importance of community and criticizing above all the book
by Ferdinand Toennies, in which he attempts to provide
a systematic justification of this heresy, I wrote "Basic
types of social rules of the game." [And, by the way, this
did not prevent the "grand old man of German sociology," in a comprehensive review of this criticism directed
against him, from referring to it as "one of the most significant contributions made until now to pure or theoretical sociology."[2]]

Max Frisch does immediately refer to his sentence as
"utopian"; but he does not in the least water it down. "A
utopia does not lose its value just because we do not live
up to it." There is no need to discuss here the sense of
wanting to, or being obliged to "live up to" a utopia of
one's own making. In my opinion, a utopia is "devalued"
or, rather, has no value from the outset, if it is clearly in
contradiction with reality.

One of the declared intentions of this newly presented
work is to show that there is a conflict with reality in the
thesis about the so-called salutary "conversion to a community."

2   See Bibliography p. 59

I. Sociology – a broad subject

The word "sociology," formed from two unhappily joined halves – one a Latin word and the other a Greek word – refers to a virtually unlimited range of themes. There are, besides, innumerable possibilities of making links with other names: sociology of religion, of economics, of knowledge, of the world of work, of the family, of art – and so on. Indeed, hardly any human activity is imaginable which is not affected by the life we share. For this reason, every branch of knowledge which deals with the human being, even if its object is the spiritual development of the individual person, inevitably has to do with social reality. However, it is obvious that not every scientific preoccupation with the human being can be called sociology. In the language of traditional philosophy: it is not the *material* object but the *formal* object that, strictly speaking, makes sociology a scientific discipline. The formal object of sociology is "the social" aspect of human reality.

However, "the social" can mean two things. By its very nature it is realized in a twofold form: for this reason there are also two clearly distinguishable forms of sociology, for which different names have been suggested. The distinction has been made between "formal" and "material" sociology [Simmel, von Wiese, Geiger]; there is the division between "sociology of society" and the "sociology of culture" [Vierkandt]; Toennies, on the other hand

– as already mentioned – sees this present book as belonging to the field of "pure or theoretical" sociology. All of these distinctions seem to me – insofar as they are at all relevant to our subject – lacking in precision.

Two Forms of Sociology

The distinction is most easily described using an analogy found in an almost forgotten book from the early years which saw the emergence of German sociology. It is certainly true that its basic conception remains, on the whole, problematic. It is also true that, from the beginning, it became discredited because the author's system of concepts was too pedantic. That is one of the reasons why colleagues in the discipline never unreservedly accepted the comprehensive *opus* or even discussed it seriously. I am referring to the four volumes published by the Swabian Albert Schäffle 1875/78. The cumbersome wordiness of the title already points to the questionable nature of the list of themes: "Structure and life of the social body. Sketch of a real anatomy, physiology, psychology of human society, with special reference to economy as social metabolism."

One thought can justifiably be taken from the many strands in the web of this book– one of, which is relevant to our present concern – without there being the slightest need to accept the thesis of the general comparability of biological and social processes. To be more precise: there is a quite definite analogy, on the basis of which the distinction that separates the two different modes of sociology in the strict sense can be named with accuracy.

It is well known that in anatomy the distinction is made between tissue and organ. Tissues are determined by the varying kinds of cell connections; there is muscle tissue, nerve tissue, skin tissue, bone tissue – and so on. Organs, on the other hand [hand, eye, heart, brain], are primarily defined by their function in the totality of the living body. They are also, at the same time, characterized by the forms of tissue which they link with one another in different ways.

If we compare this distinction between tissue and organ with the distinction between the two fundamentally different kinds of sociology this does not amount, strictly speaking, to a comparison between the social and the biological. This has nothing to do with what was once sometimes referred to as "organic sociology." The comparison and analogy in question is something quite different: namely, the biological *distinction* between tissue and organ on the one hand and, on the other hand, the *distinction* between social tissue forms and social organs. We are concerned with the purely logical analogy between two different conceptual relationships. One might want to discuss whether to speak of "social histology" and "social organology" is an apt use of words, but as long as it is clear what is, and what is not, meant by this terminology, no harm is done. What is meant by this distinction is that in human intercourse the manifold structured relationships between individuals are to be distinguished from the social organs which are defined by their functions [family, state, church, army, business – and so on]. Only in these social organs are the interpersonal forms of bonding realized – each in its own peculiar way. And just as biological histology is not sufficient for the understanding of the body as a complete organism or of the individual organs, so even the most accurate knowledge of the different forms in the web of relationships does not yield an understanding of concrete human society or of its organs which are defined by their function. This is where, for example, there is a fundamental lack of a sociology which understands itself exclusively or primarily as a "theory of relationships," in the way in which, however, it was representative of social science in Germany for decades between the two world wars.[3] The characteristic statement that sees the state as a particular "mixture" of mutual relationships and oppositional relationships is grotesquely inadequate. Such a "definition" is just as meaningless as it would be for a biologist to describe the organism or the organ as a "mixture" arising out of the different ways that cells are linked. Thus "histology," whether biological or sociological, is not enough. And yet it is indispensable for understanding the complete reality of both organic and social life. Sociological thinking can also possibly fail to reflect reality if it too hastily – for example, in consideration of political and social concerns – turns its attention to the "concrete situation of society" *without* taking into account forms and processes in interpersonal relations; just as in the biological sphere, there can be "bad" distortions in the social fabric which could only be detected by "histological" study.

This area of "histology" – which, admittedly, represents only a preliminary introduction to a comprehensive understanding of social reality – is where the theme of "social rules of the game" has its place. This theme is what defines the limits and claims of the current book.

What is meant by a "social rule of the game"?

Three concrete examples. The first case: a critical social report tells how in a business firm difficulties arose from a

3   See Leopold von Wiese, Allgemeine Soziologie

typist wanting to be treated in the office as a "lady"; during the office dance she was treated this way as a matter of course, even by the boss. Second case: two friends are soldiers in the same unit, one as an officer and the other as a private soldier. Naturally, one man cannot expect to be treated as a friend when in service as a soldier any more than the other man can expect to be respected as a superior in their lives outside the army. Third case: years ago my eldest son participated in one of my seminars as a student. We enjoyed conspiring, in a quite serious endeavor to find ways around using the familiar "Du" form; thus the other participants, mildly amused, heard me refer to the "honorable speaker" who had just delivered himself of some not altogether unproblematic ideas. At least we did not hold with the customary practice of businessmen in Bremen, where father and son in the business environment used the formal "Sie" in addressing one another.

It is already clear from these random snapshots what is meant by the expression "social rules of the game": namely, the various norms of behavior which are spontaneously followed, given a particular type of human intercourse. It may be mentioned in passing – by way of a perhaps devious anticipation – that these snapshots are already an introduction to the three basic kinds of social relationships. These will presently be dealt with in detail.

The question about whether there is anything binding in such rules of the game is not easy to answer. At first sight, the term "rule of the game" broadly suggests a quite low level of commitment. But we need to remember that even a game – whether tennis or chess – would be impossible without rules which every player accepts as

binding. Moreover, in normal everyday language partners in a collective agreement are referred to as the opposing social "players." And the "Handwörterbuch der
Soziologie" (Pocket book of Sociology), which appeared
as early as 1931, was already referring to the "liberal rule
of the game" or the "rule that applied to the economic
playing field." One hesitates to attribute to these norms
of behavior any strict "moral" binding force. However,
we cannot refrain from thinking of this mutual human
behavior in terms of a norm or, more clearly, in terms of
justice. The question, therefore, is whether corresponding
to each of the different forms of social intercourse there
is a particular way of being just. But an adequate answer
to this question can only be expected when each of the
different forms of social intercourse has been described
and given a name.

Basic forms of association

"To associate with one another," as can be seen in the
brothers Grimm "Deutsches Wörterbuch" [German Dic-
tionary], has for centuries in our language meant "being
bound to one another by an inner bond." Accordingly, this
not altogether old technical term in sociology should only
be applied to human relationships which are based on
mutual affirmation by the partners, and in what follows
we will retain the term. The chance gathering of people
waiting together at a bus stop is not an association in the
strict sense; to be accurate, they are not waiting in "association." But perhaps in the group there are parents with
their children – therefore four or five people who have "an
inner bond" with one another: and now they are, in fact,
"associated" with one another on the way home.

The distinction between association in the narrow, strict sense and any other kinds of groupings is something we are confronted with on a daily basis, although not everyone knows the distinction – which, in any case, is not easy to draw. If one were to present a group of students – for instance, sociology students – with a list of groupings which we see every day on the street or on television and were to ask them to find and identify the real "associations," the results would probably be quite varied. The following could be the list of groups: a football team at training; an orchestra performing a concert; a family having its midday meal; a boxing match; a church service; a whipped up crowd wildly applauding or protesting; a reception to celebrate the birthday of a politician; a street conflict between demonstrators and police; a village market; a military parade.

Probably the family, the church service, and the football team would generally be considered as associative. Some would perhaps see the applauding or protesting crowd in this light; if everyone keeps on calling out the same things it may be thought that they feel themselves united. We will deal later in detail with this characteristic misinterpretation: the confusion of similarity in external behavior with mutual affirmation. Perhaps this might correspond to the participants' own self-deception. But it would be more significant, if also not very surprising, if neither the orchestra nor the military formation were to be seen as genuine forms of social relationships; but, in fact, this mutual affirmation is normally realized here also, although admittedly in a very special way which constitutes it as a form of real association. And with regard to receptions and markets, which are probably not considered as instances of association, there is again mutual

acceptance of the partners, which does make the social relationship, in the average case, into a kind of association
– a particular kind of association, and one which is not always easy to identify.

It is obvious that the mutual affirmation of people
who are joined in a social relationship can be realized in
very different forms. This can only be made plausible if
we present certain basic facts for consideration.

Every human being, in his concrete existence, represents [first] something *general*, something which he has in
common with others, perhaps with all human beings. At
the same time [second] each human being is an *individual*
who lives his own separate, special existence which he can
share with no one else, no matter how much else he has
in common with others that binds him to them. And
[third] every human being is qualitatively *special*, not just
"one" beside others, each of whom is also "one"; each is
not only "not the other" but is also *other* than the other;
that means: in every individual the "general" aspect of
being human is realized in a unique and unrepeatable
way.

Each of these structural elements can give a social
grouping its peculiar character. The "general" provides
the possibility and guarantee of all agreement and common ground; the corresponding form of association is the
community. "Individuality," on the other hand, is an essential aspect of *society*; while, as a form of association, it
presupposes mutuality of affirmation, at the same time it
expressly makes room for individual interest, the private
sphere, and self-preservation. The third form of association is *organization*. It centres on the "special" aspect of the
people, driving them to complement one another, to
achieve a common goal, and to share the work involved.

In summary, those are the three basic forms of association; corresponding to them are the various rules of the game which we must now deal with in detail. For the sake of clarity we shall, in what follows, stick to the meaning of the terms as defined above – in spite of the fact that the terms are also used differently in other contexts [for example, "European community," "The individual and society" – and so forth].

In concrete social reality, of course, these three basic forms of association – community, society, organization – never exist in a "pure" form. Just as, in reality, a human person is made up of the general, the individual, and the special, so every existing social structure is determined by all three structural elements. But that does not mean, for example, that the family is not as a rule *primarily* a community, although it also involves division of labor and room for the private sphere. And the military unit is subject first and foremost to the rules of the game of an organization; but without respect for the personal dignity of the individual and without the community element found in camaraderie it would be inhuman.

At this point a precautionary comment is in order which takes up again what has already been said about the limits of this idea. It is obvious that, however accurate the things already said about the community character of family life, nothing has been said about things which are perhaps far more essential. The family as a household, as an economic consumer group; its biological reproductive function; the religious foundations and values inculcated – all of that, of course, lies beyond the scope of "histological" discussion. The same applies also for all concrete social structures which, with a view toward clarification by examples, will be referred to in the following pages.

II. Community

Rules of the game for a community

A community as a social grouping has two distinguishing features: on the one hand, the mutual affirmation of the members of the group, and on the other hand, the assertion of that which is common to the members of the group. Both of these characteristics, as is immediately obvious, are connected in a special way and are even disposed to promote and help one another to grow. It is hardly possible to conceive of one without the other.

But there is a type of common sharing without mutual affirmation. All in the grouping may, perhaps even vehemently and with passion, do the same thing without mutual affirmation; of course, if one looks more closely, the common sharing turns out to be merely apparent. All of this applies to actions by the "masses" in which there is no form of social relationship at all. We will deal with this in more detail later.

But there can also be a social relationship based on mutual affirmation, the core of which is not what the members have in common; this is what characterizes "society," in which the assertion of the interests of the individual is linked with the mutual affirmation of partners and is therefore also a form of genuine association. This will be the theme of the next chapter.

In the community, everything that limits the

community or could destroy it – above all, the interest of the individual, even when justified in itself – has to yield. The interest in question is not necessarily concerned with material advantage – although, in English, capital gain is not by chance called "interest," just as, on the other hand, the rules of the game for a community are specially characterized by the fact that it is not usual for a person to demand interest for a loan given to a friend. But, as I have said, the self-interest, the assertion of which could destroy the community or make it impossible, can be directed to quite different things: to position and prestige, for example, to power, to pleasure; psychology speaks of "asocial gaining of pleasure." And precisely this sphere, perhaps veiled in self-deception, is where the endangerments to community life, both in marriage and family, are to be found.

Friends are able and willing to share, and they communicate with one another. The "star" and the "prima donna" types, for whom the others are primarily "audience," only *seem* to live in a form of community. In his fine book on friendship, the Cistercian abbot Aelred of Rievaulx [1110-1167] says that a true friend does not seek any advantage from a friendship except for the good that is contained in friendship as such.

Here the "surrender," even of a personal interest to which one is entitled, cannot be expected, except on the basis of an inner attitude which can only be called love – insofar as by this term we understand something which is a relationship other than one based purely on justice. With good reason it has frequently been said that justice separates people rather than joining them together. In a social relationship based solely on justice people deal with each other as individuals "having a justifiable demand

and needing to fulfil a requirement."[4] Thomas Aquinas writes: "Justice without mercy is cruelty."[5] But here mercy obviously stands for the love which is expressly distinguished from justice – love which, of course, is not the same as sentimentality.

But where love in such a sense joins people together, there is, of course, directness and intimacy in interpersonal intercourse; and everything that stands in the way of this directness is alien to the life of the community. Disturbances and hindrances of this kind could be due to the accepted forms of behavior or to the introduction of a third party or of a technical apparatus. The relationship between people joined in community knows no formality or ceremony; they choose whatever is the shortest route from one to the other. They use first names in speaking to one another, and in German the informal "Du" is used. Thus the transition from mere acquaintanceship to friendship is usually accompanied by expressly relinquishing the [German formal] "Sie" form which previously had been taken for granted, whereas terminating a friendship is usually expressed in the conscious reverting to exact observance of social forms.

It is true that the distancing potential of official codes of behavior has been gradually diminished over the course of time. At the end of the seventeenth century it was characteristic of court etiquette to speak to a person of higher rank in the third person, but by 1750, "Sie" [second person plural] is the polite form generally used, and today, in urban life, this form has lost all trace of indirectness – so

4   O. von Nell-Breuning, Die soziale Enzyklika. Cologne, 1932, p. 224
5   In Matth. 5,2

that even in friendship between men it is the normal mode of address.

The rules of the game for a community likewise normally exclude, as I said, the introduction of a human or technical intermediary. When we can, we communicate with a friend directly, and not through a third person. A love letter is, where possible, written by hand. It is true that the typewriter, not unlike the code of social behavior, has largely lost its distancing effect – so that, in the meantime, the technical apparatus does not remove the character of a quite personal communication even from a love letter. Of course, one is hardly likely to use a dictaphone.

From the intimacy and directness which we take for granted in community life it is no great step to wholehearted openness. But this is where we need to speak of the limits to the validity of this form of association which now hove into view.

"To have no secrets from one another" is a sign of a specially intimate bond. People meet one another with no veil between them, so to speak, unarmed and without a mask. "All doors are open." But here there is not just the "risk of being ridiculous," a risk which which Helmut Plessner has said is feasible only in a human relationship of the greatest intimacy. More serious, it seems to me, is the loss of "chastity" of the soul in such a surrender of its innermost life. This loss can be as harmful for the life of the individual as it can for the life of the community. This is probably the thrust of Nietzsche's well-known statement about the community that makes things "common" and of the realistic warning that "familiarity breeds contempt." And Romano Guardini knew very well what he was talking about – on the basis of his experience of romantic communities connected with youth organizations

– when he wrote in one of his early essays[6] that uncondi-
tional dedication to a community ends in destruction of
the individual person.

The exclusive nature of the "community" ideal certainly has no criterion that could provide the possibility
of a corrective to such destructive unconditionality. It is
far more necessary to find a vantage point from which it
is possible to comprehend the totality of the forms of association which are appropriate to man as a "political
being."

6   Möglichkeiten und Grenzen der Gemeinschaft

III. Society

"Society" outlawed

The previous chapter ended with a warning against absolutizing community. What follows must begin with a warning against the downgrading of society as a form of association. – Before we can speak about this form we need first to look critically at the objections which have been raised against it.

The downgrading of society would seem to be limited to German speaking countries. In this there is, of course, a fairly long history composed of many different strands. In the very earliest attempt – claimed to be the first attempt – undertaken to define the meaning of "society," this devaluation, considered as a response to the French Revolution, was clearly formulated by Lorenz von Stein [1815-1890]. Von Stein was born in North Germany. He then taught, principally in Vienna, as professor of "political economy." He has been called the "Founder of Sociology in Germany."[7] From the very beginning, the community has here been seen positively as a contrast to society, whose principle is "interest." Community is seen as "individual persons being there for one another within a plurality."[8] A

---

7   Staatslexikon, edited by the Görres-Gesellschaft. 6th edition, Freiburg 1962, vol.7, column 677
8   L. von Stein, Der Begriff der Gesellschaft und die soziale

good generation later Ferdinand Toennies will take up this idea and radicalize it. For him, society is something absolutely "pathological" and a symptom of decay.[9] People "socially" bound together, he says, are not "really" connected with one another; instead, society is "a mere being side by side" of "essentially separate" individual persons.[10] It has only the "appearance of a living together";[11] it is "potential enmity" and "hidden warfare"[12]; it lacks warmth and it makes even women "cold hearted."[13]

The list of objections and accusations must, for the sake of clarity, be rounded out. Society, says Toennnies, is based on egotism, "on the desire and fear of the individual person, whose will, in truth, has nothing to do with any other person than oneself"; it is founded on the reasoned calculation of what is useful and advantageous.[14] In conclusion, a sentence in which Toennies summarizes everything negative that, for him, is connected with the idea of "society": it involves, he is convinced, a form of living together in which "each person is there for all, each seems to value the others as his equal, whereas in truth each one thinks only of the self and, in opposition to all the others, endeavors to assert his own importance and to work to his own advantage.[15]

Geschichte der Französischen Revolution bis 1830, p. VII, p. XIV

9   F. Toennies, Soziologische Studien und Kritiken. Vol.I, p. 43, p. 71
10   Gemeinschaft und Gesellschaft. 6/7. Edition, p. 39
11   Ibid., p. 5
12   Ibid., p. 52
13   Ibid., p. 162
14   Soziologische Studien und Kritiken, vol. I, p. 32
15   Gemeinschaft und Gesellschaft, p. 53

In this definite rejection, one hears as overtones, so to speak, still more objections which are likewise worth mentioning because their effect, too, extends way beyond the individual author. One cannot help hearing the overtone of emotional antipathy towards the city as a place of social life. Corresponding to this is the distrust of all "public" life, which is seen in negative contrast to romantically transfigured family life: "All intimate, private living together that excludes others is what is understood as life in a community.[16] Finally, in the distinction between community and society the antithesis between "formerly" and "now" is implied, "formerly" being understood as the time prior to "middle class society" and "now" being understood as "middle class society." Tönnies characterizes it as the most striking form of the manifold phenomena which are summarized in the sociological concept of society."[17] "Community is old, society new, both in name and in what they are."[18]

Should one try to reduce to one all-inclusive formula all the types of rejection we have named – some of them very strange when they appear in an extreme form – it could be something like this: what is wrong with society is that it is not community. –Over against this, the aim will be to show in the following pages that these objections are either wide of the mark or are not real objections at all.

Society and its rules of the game

Mutually affirmed commitment which is crystallized in the accentuated individuality of the partners: both of these

16 Gemeinschaft und Gesellschaft, p. 3f.
17 Handwörterbuch der Soziologie, p. 191
18 Gemeinschaft und Gesellschaft, p. 4

attributes of the form of association called "society" – by contrast to those of community – clearly do not fit together without problems. There is no question of their reinforcing one another or working together for one another's development; instead, they seem to be almost incompatible with one another. "Society" as a form of association, in fact, naturally consists of a strained relationship. Its structural features are to be thought of as linked with one another not by a neutral "and" but by an almost explosive "in spite of": mutually affirmed commitment of partners despite the individuality they simultaneously stress. Community comes about of itself; society, on the other hand, demands of the partners a special kind of effort and powers of resistance in the face of an almost natural explosive force.

However, it is not just any kind of need for systematic completeness that has us speaking of society as a form of social relationship. The need is based both on insight into the nature of the human person living in a social relationship with others and on evaluation of empirical reality. We have now to speak of "society" under these two aspects, which it is not always possible to keep separate from one another.

Regarding "individuality" as the core of "society," it can be said more precisely that the human being is not only, like all other beings, something separate, something apart from everything that is not the self; rather, the individuality of the human being means that it is not a something but a someone, an I myself, a person; and that means a "world in itself," something complete in itself and for itself, a being that exists for the sake of its own fulfilment and perfection. Personal beings cannot "figure as 'parts' of a whole."[19]

19 D. von Hildebrand, Metaphysik der Gemeinschaft, p. 22

Precisely on the basis of being capable of self-determination the human being can, indeed, "surrender" himself and become a member of a community, but at the same time his being a person requires that his "private" sphere be respected, and it is the foundation of his claim to all else to which he is entitled. Naturally, such a claim presupposes independence. A child lives at first in the community as in a nest. But when one day a son is growing up and asserts his right to his own personal sphere – for instance, his right to have private correspondence – it does not necessarily mean that the family ceases to be primarily a community way of life; but something new appears and the "limits of community" hove into view. But the health of the shared life in the family will perhaps be tested by the way this new and different element – the social rule of the game – is also allowed for.

But no one lives exclusively in the family, in a circle of friends or in a religious community. It is inevitable that one lives also amongst strangers, or at least amongst people with whom one has no close relationship. We lead a "public" life, which Toennies defines as the "sphere of society" – and in this he is quite right. And yet it is incomprehensible that he could label this form of living together as something "pathological," as a mere appearance of living together, as "potential enmity" – because as he sees it, in reality everyone calculatingly thinks only of himself and of what is to his advantage.

In what follows, the example of two representative forms of "social" life – more precisely, the contractual relationship and social intercourse with the outside world – will help to make clear that "society" *can* in truth be a form of genuine social relationship, i.e. one based on mutual affirmation, and in fact normally *is*.

The contractual relationship

Ferdinand Toennies speaks, somewhat contemptuously – but he is also wide of the mark – of the "market," in which "the nature of society presents itself as if in a concave mirror."[20] The market can, indeed, be understood as a network of contractual relationships, as the place where interests are balanced out by give and take. Every contract, whether concerning a sale or a publishing project, is based on the principle *do ut des* [I give so that you will give – DF], i.e. on the principle of direct payment for something. The choice of the contractual form has no other meaning for the individual than to establish and safeguard the basis for his own claim and the partner's obligation.

In a community there is normally no contract. Some contrasting examples will illustrate this. The "marriage contract" as a means of regulating legal property rights of the married couple is not aimed at defining the interests of one partner over against those of the other partner but rather at securing their common rights against the possible claim of a third party, such as creditors or heirs. In the context of work, the community character of the relationship dictates [or used to dictate, not so long ago] and takes for granted that there is no contract, especially on farms and in family businesses. But in the modern labor "market" characterized by the "commercializing of the workforce" [G. Briefs] the rules of the game relating to society exclusively prevail: the mutual interests of employer and employee are exactly defined in the wage agreement, and none of the "social opponents" is prepared to give or

20 Gemeinschaft und Gesellschaft, p. 51

demand anything beyond what the contract requires nor to waive anything to which the contract gives a right. Advertisements do speak on occasion of the "hospitality" of a hotel or airline; but no one is fooled into thinking that, in this context, "guest" and "host" are anything more than interested parties. By contrast, a house guest staying with friends shares, as a member of a community, whatever goods belong to the community.

The nature of contract and market is most clearly seen in a sale contract, where the real formal and material causes are defined by striving for the greatest possible gain. Both partners are clear about this. And even the expression which has now become usual in the salesman's vocabulary – "serving the customer" – leaves no doubt about the fact that not only the goods but also this "service" has to be paid for. What is fundamentally common to all contractually determined relationships between people – in the ideal case, between *strangers*, as Toennies notes – is here most nakedly exposed: it is crystallized in the emphasis on the individual interests of the partners who, not without reason, are sometimes also called "treaty opponents."

But it is now time to speak of the other side of the coin – the second structural element: namely, the mutual affirmation ("in spite of everything") of the partners, through which the contractual relationship becomes a genuine, and only then genuine, form of association as a "society."

A contract does not at all amount to a declaration of love; but it does mean that the partners "get on." "Good faith" is even the legally formulated and binding principle in law when a contract is being signed. The contract is based on the mutual self-interest of the partners; but both wish, unless they are quite simply swindlers, to achieve their own advantage while accepting the condition that the other also is to be given his due. This is precisely the essence of a contractual relationship, namely, that the individual asserts himself without wanting to disadvantage the other partner. At first sight that might seem a mere requirement: that's the way it "ought" to be, but is it really like that? I think we can say that observance of contracts – which is also rightly called "social virtue as such" – does happen on a daily basis in the market. And not only the formal validity of the contract once it is entered into but also the "equivalence principle" regarding the content – such that there is equality between what is given and what is received – is normally respected in the practical balancing of interests. Only a total cynic would contest this or explain it away as "fear of the law." What matters here is not so much a consciously fostered or even openly declared ethical attitude, but what is practised in fact.

Even in civil proceedings in court – certainly the most extreme form of balancing of interests – the parties do naturally want to defend their interests, but not at any cost. Whether it is expressed or not, they accept the condition that the other party should receive its due. The parties want to be given "*their* right," but in wanting "their *right*" they are in fact limiting their claim. The balancing of interests through court proceedings is no uplifting sight for anyone with a romantic notion of community and it is, in reality, incompatible with life in a community. However, one cannot deny the profound and gratifying distinction between a civil action and the rule of force.

In this combination of defense, on the one hand, of one's interests and, on the other hand, of good faith, of acknowledging the equality principle and therefore acknowledging and affirming the partner, an attitude is manifested which we can characterize in a special sense as justice as distinct from love. If love says: what belongs to me must belong to all – justice says: to each his own [which naturally also includes: to me what is mine]. At this point we should recall that Thomas Aquinas added a second sentence to the one already quoted about justice without mercy being cruelty: "Mercy without justice is the mother of dissolution."[21] It is clear that justice alone cannot maintain order in the world, but it remains the metal core of human co-existence. The assertion of one's own individual interest is what distinguishes society from community. But the mutual affirmation of the partners through the faithful observance of a contract and through acknowledgement of the equality principle distinguishes justice from injustice, the partner in a contract from the criminal, and society as a form of genuine social relationship from Machiavellian brute force in which everyone hunts down what is to his own advantage however and wherever he finds it. Naturally, such brute force can prevail precisely under the mask of good faith, just as boundless egoism can hide behind the deceptive appearance of community life.

Social intercourse with strangers and "social" association

"As soon as one comes in contact with society one removes the key from one's heart and puts it in one's pocket; those who leave it in the lock are idiots." That does not sound, the first time one hears it, particularly social. And to one who did not know that it stems from a person

21 In Matth. 5,2

who was [for the most part] happy to converse – Goethe – the sentence could seem to be an expression of a crass individualism that seeks anything but society. And yet it applies precisely to what is now about to be said – even if we are to consider only one of the two structural elements which determine the "social" mode of intercourse with strangers and which are to be thought of as joined together in an explosively tense relationship. It is the element of individuality, which does not, as in the contractual relationship, concern material interest but the right to having a private sphere, distance, the possibility of avoiding intimacy.

In a community people want to be as close to one another as possible. In social intercourse, the reverse is the case: no one "comes too close" to the other. By contrast to the easy nature of community life, the point of formality and "etiquette" is to avoid and to impede any breakdown of distance. Helmuth Plessner speaks in his book "Grenzen der Gemeinschaft" of the "longing for a mask behind which directness disappears." That is perhaps an extreme formulation, but the author is surely right when he calls the formality of social intercourse "the path to invulnerability," a means of defense, therefore, against invasion of one's privacy.

We are still speaking exclusively of *one* element of relationships in society – of course, a constitutive element: individuality, self-preservation, reserve, and distance. And we understand, naturally, that it is said that this form of social intercourse "places the person firmly on the periphery."[22] But this objection is not necessarily valid. Social "conversation" normally does not mean a "declaring of

22   D. von Hildebrand, Metaphysik der Gemeinschaft, p. 143f.

oneself" between the partners, but rather it is marked by the factual taking precedence over the personal. But there is, in principle, no limit set to what "facts" are spoken of.

With good reason it has also been noted that this form of social intercourse has, in some respects, features which remind us of the market situation. The once famous booklets about "the art of pleasing at court" speak, not by chance, of the *grand commerce du monde*. This gives Toennies further cause to criticize "conventional" social intercourse, in which "the most important rule," by analogy with the balancing of interests in the market place, is an "exchange of words and favors."[23] There is, in fact, a marked difference between the presents exchanged between friends and those which are "exchanged" in society. In this latter case one feels obliged to return the "favour" [a visit or an invitation] so as to cancel whatever obligation has arisen as soon as possible. On the basis of a kind of "payment" the partners are then "quits," i.e. their individuality is confirmed and preserved; there is no longer any debt between them.

Payment, above all through money, is indeed the best way to avoid being direct and to make any purely social togetherness impossible. In this, we again see what an explosive mixture it is where both elements of the form of association we have called "society" are joined together. The danger of individualistic dissolution is never excluded once and for all. Kierkegaard's sarcastically drawn portrait hits the nail on the head: "So it is your principle never to accept anything without paying money for it. Money is the best means to exclude any personal relationship. You become very uncomfortable when people ...

23 Gemeinschaft und Gesellschaft, p. 53

seek a personal relationship with you which is not measurable by money."[24]

Now that enough has been said exclusively about one of the two elements which constitute society as a form of association – as well as about the accompanying danger of its dissolution through individualism – at last we must focus on the second element, the mutual affirmation, which is possible despite everything.

We could mention here at the beginning Schopenhauer's acerbic parable of the two porcupines, where the need for warmth brings these curious animals together, whereas the mutual annoyance caused by their spikes immediately drives them apart again until they ultimately find "a moderate distance from one another which makes things tolerable between them." The moral of the story: that's exactly the way it is in human society. "The moderate distance which they finally settle on and which makes it possible for them to be together is politeness and good manners." Schiller, who, much more than Goethe, fitted in easily at court, spoke positively about "society." In a letter to Christian Gottfried Körner [13.2.1793] he speaks of the laws of "good tone." He means by this old-fashioned expression the "ease of social intercourse." "The first law is: respect another's freedom; the second: show your own freedom." And then he mentions English dance, which is composed of many complicated moves ... an apt image of the freedom one claims for oneself and respects in another."

It is the relationship of these two elements to one another and in contrast to one another – clear preservation of one's own sphere and respect for the partner – that constitutes, or *should* constitute what is peculiar to social

24 Kierkegaard, Entweder-Oder, Jena 1911/13, vol. 2, pp. 84f.

intercourse and dealings with strangers and makes them to be truly human forms of co-existence.

Justice, insofar as it is distinguished from love, is, as we have said, the virtue which corresponds to the contractual balancing of interests. The hallmark of social intercourse could be summed up in the word "tact." "Tact" means not entering another person's private sphere, not foisting one's own private concerns on another, and yet at the same time taking an interest in one's neighbor and respecting his own independent dignity.

By contrast, the radical view of community which sees community as the only valid ideal of social intercourse has, not without reason, been called the "ethic of tactlessness."

A late form of social intercourse

"Society" as a form of association is "more difficult" and presupposes a higher level of maturity of consciousness than life in a community. That seems to be the reason why "society" in the life of the individual as well as in social culture as a whole is a late phenomenon.

Relationships in society and its particular forms are foreign to a child. A child cannot relate to strangers and unfamiliar people as such; the child either avoids the stranger altogether or includes him, for instance as an uncle, in the intimate sphere of the family. If the child addresses everybody in the familiar way [the "Du" form], this has nothing to do with any limitation in the child's vocabulary; it is rooted, rather, in its inability to grasp the function of the two forms of address and to distinguish the ones to be addressed by "Du" from those to be addressed by "Sie." It is not yet possible for the child to

accept a stranger or to affirm him without wishing immediately to make him into an intimate. Precisely this is the
basis for the existence of the *enfant terrible* we all know [the
chance guest at table is made privy to embarrassing family circumstances or is questioned about his own private
life – and so on.]

Learning to be just and tactful, to be fair and to show
respect to a person whom one cannot love is exactly what
it means to be adult. The aim of meaningful education of
children can hardly be anything else but to make them capable of linking the preservation of their own individuality with acknowledgement of that of the other person –
and that means understanding and practicing the rules of
the game in society. Whoever has not learnt this, remains,
although perhaps fairly old in years, an *enfant terrible*.

Ethnology shows that "primitive" tribes living in iso-
lation have attitudes to relationships which largely correspond to those of children. Facts like bartering,
neutralizing of the market area, exchange of goods
through guest presents, whereby a contractual and therefore social process unfolds in what has the appearance of
a community form – all these and some further manifes-
tations of the "primitive" social life seem to suggest difficulties in initiation into the rules of the game in society
which are not easy to overcome. But in this respect the
concerns are so complicated and controversial that the
non-specialist has to be satisfied with brief pointers. In
any case, it can be said with some certainty that the possibility of a "socially" regulated bond, in which above all
the individuality of the stranger is acknowledged, will be
long in coming. "Innumerable facts gathered from studies
of antiquity and ethnology indicate that people of another
tribe are not at all seen as possible friends until a relatively

high level of development has been achieved."[25] In his small book about diplomats Jules Cambon, a diplomat himself, tells a true story which is characteristic of this phenomenon.[26] A tribal prince of the Tuareg who became a prisoner of war of the French was taken through a World Exhibition and was asked afterwards what amazed him the most. The chief from the Sahara mentioned neither the Eiffel Tower nor the Ferris wheel but the fact that one could mingle with so many strangers without being armed. Leaving aside the fact that this highly intelligent observer must not have noticed the more or less hidden presence of the very well-armed police, one has to admire his perspicuity in realizing and naming what constitutes "society" as a form of social relationship – one could almost say, of middle-class society. We could, of course, wonder whether we are not, today, on the point of now losing what has been achieved.

On the other hand, absolutizing "society" is just as repugnant to reality as any kind of radical attitude to community; it is probably even more destructive because it threatens to uproot the individual from the nourishing soil of community life, which is the only basis on which even the "social" form of relating can be "learnt."[27] Ferdinand Toennies gives a wittily formulated portrait of a "dealer" and a typical educated person: "Not belonging anywhere, a traveler, familiar with foreign customs and arts, having no love or respect for those of a given country, speaking several languages, glib and devious, suave and accommodating, and yet always with an eye to his own

25 Th. Geiger, Gestalten der Gesellung, p. 94
26 J. Cambon, Le diplomate, Paris 1926
27 A. Vierkandt, Gesellschaftslehre, p. 315

advantage, he moves back and forth quickly and smoothly; he changes character and his way of thinking [his faith or opinions] like fashion in clothes; he carries one thing or the other from one territory to the other; he mixes and balances, using the old and the new to his advantage."[28] While this is a masterfully drawn caricature, it corresponds exactly to what can happen in extreme cases.

28 Gemeinschaft und Gesellschaft, p. 164

IV. Organization

Organization as a basic form of social living

When we speak of "organization" we are not at all [perhaps even deliberately not] referring to a particular form of "relating to one another socially," i.e. to a form of human relationship; and to speak of an "organizational relationship" between people seems at first sight to be completely absurd. Instead, what comes to mind is the original meaning of the word "organ" derived from the Greek *organon* [= tool]. And in fact "organization" means, just like the linguistically related biological concept "organism," the organs operating together as a working unit towards achieving a particular goal with each performing its own distinct function. The crucial element in the concept "organization" is the end or purpose it "serves" and which determines the structure and the way in which the members collaborate. The members, for their part, are not focusing on one another as individuals, but first and foremost on the end and purpose of their common endeavor. When a once particularly influential sociologist says that organization means, "arranging people in a particular relationship of distance to one another"[29] he is not identifying the essential point. Organizing means, instead, as I

29 L. von Wiese, Systematische Soziologie in Deutschland, p. 164

have already suggested, making people into an active unit in which each individual, performing his own special function, is bound together with others – also exercising their specific functions – where they complement one another and share the work.

However, it is only natural that in this way interpersonal relationships are formed which are clearly different from all other types of social relationships. We are dealing here with a particular form of human bonding which is to be described as a separate, discrete form of social relationship and is not reducible to any other form or to be explained by it. As soon as they join an organization, people – insofar as and as soon as they are active as members – do not see themselves primarily as friends [although they could be in fact] nor as individuals who have respect for one another, not as interested partners in a contractual relationship , but as what? As "functionaries"! The core of the mode of association "organization" is neither, as in the community, the common element that binds them together, nor, as in society, their individuality, but the special quality that distinguishes them from the others , whereby in the best possible scenario the special subjective bent and abilities on the one hand and on the other hand the special nature of the function to be exercised converge; as the saying goes, 'the right man in the right place.'

But now, by definition, an association of persons should be characterized by mutually affirmed solidarity. But perhaps one can ask how this works with organizations and whether it can be expected in the average case. The answer to this not unreasonable question is as follows: if we are not dealing with the exceptional case of a group of people brought together by external pressures, but, let us say, with an orchestra, a football team, a technical or industrial firm, then there is indeed such mutual affirmation, also in average circumstances. Of course, this does not have to come about in any conscious or emotional way. What is important is that it influences practical behavior. In the factual acceptance by the individual of his position in the fundamental plan which an organization has set out for itself there is clear agreement with such a working unit as a whole and also an affirmation of a bond between the active members. It is important – and quite sufficient – that the individual is aware of collaborating with others for achieving a common goal and that he himself freely carries out his particular function. If these conditions are fulfilled, one can logically conclude that there is a mutual affirmation which is one of the structural elements of all types of social relationships.

It is clear to everyone that in the ordinary way of speaking and thinking about "organization" there is much that has little or nothing to do with the concept presented here. Professional associations and unions are called organizations; the editors of the Handwörterbuch der Soziologie of 1931 considered that the term "organization" meant nothing but the "shape and forms of associations, societies etc."[30] And a scientific monograph on "The fundamentals of organization theory" begins with the sentence: "Organization is the quintessence of measures which ..."[31]

And so in what follows, what is meant by "organization" is this: a fundamental form of association which is

30 J. Plenge, Acht Glossen zum Betrieb der Gesellschaftslehre, p. 163
31 R. Erdmann, Grundlagen einer Organisationslehre

crystallized in the special character of the members and is based on their mutual affirmation.

Rules of the game of the organization

I am returning to the case I have already mentioned of the two friends who are soldiers in the same military unit, one as an officer and the other as a private soldier. Let us suppose that in a particular situation the officer is faced with the impertinent demand, or even the temptation, to free his friend – for the sake of friendship – from an unpleasant or even dangerous task. How would he decide, as a good officer who affirms the aims and purposes of military service? What would it be his duty to say to himself or to his friend? This is where the rules of the game pertaining to the organization would come into play. The meaning of his answer to the demand or temptation would have to be: you and I, as soldiers, are part of a set of functions, all of which serve to protect our country. What is important is that this goal be achieved. That means that each of us, in his role, fulfils the duty assigned to him. Naturally we are friends and remain so. But as long as we are "serving," our relationship is defined primarily by the different functions we perform in the military setup and not by our friendship.

It is not difficult to see the characteristic change in the rules of behavior when an interpersonal relationship is confronted by the requirements of the organization. The cohesion of a football team, for instance, depends to a large extent on the need for camaraderie. But as soon as the game is on, the completely different rules of the game come into force; suddenly the friend is the "outside left" or the "man in goal." Even the inner relationship between the individuals changes when they are concerned with a goal which they can only achieve by collaboration.

In an amateur orchestra whose members may all be friends with one another, the relationship between them naturally changes as soon as the music begins; immediately one is no longer primarily a friend but an "oboist" or "viola player"; in other words, suddenly the organization's rules of the game are in force, all the more so as the players are committed to the work they are to produce in common. The passionate outbursts of anger that greet the careless or ill-prepared colleague have nothing to do with personal enmity. The friendship between them all is in no way threatened. The "organizational" row is normally situated on a different level; it does not at all mean that people are personally at loggerheads, but only that they are insisting on the perfect performance of their function.

The rules of the game for an organization could fittingly be described with one single word: "membership," which quite literally is to be understood as "being a member as others are [of a body]."

That the rules of the game of an organization are not always without conflict with those governing a community or a society will already be clear from the examples cited. Also the split between duty and inclination, which is often described in sociological literature, is sometimes the split between the rules of organization and those of community. The possibility, significant in practice, of *infringement* of the rules of behavior in an organization occurs when, in the apportioning of functions or granting freedom from them, a yardstick other than that of ability and suitability is applied. In the already mentioned writing of the medieval abbot Aelred of Rievaulx we find the comment that Christ did not make his favorite disciple

John head of the Church; and so the leader of an "organization" must also confer offices and functions not on the basis of friendship but according to competence.

There is the possibility of conflict of a quite different kind where the mode of functioning of an organization with regard to human relationships becomes the norm even when the rules of the game for a community or a society should be observed. Clearly there is a type of person who tends to see all social relationships as a kind of fulfilling of a function and to treat them as such. These persons are always, so to speak, "on duty" – even in their family life and in everyday social intercourse. A particular form of "Prussianism" has, more or less justifiably, been characterized in this way. We can happily pass over that. But there is a surprising current relevance of this phenomenon to conditions prevailing in political totalitarianism, which clearly has the tendency to treat the people in its sphere of influence, exclusively and without exception, as functionaries serving the aims of the state. According to its fundamental, radically collectivist theory, community, or social, or any "private" relationships between individuals are of no importance, if they are even not to be seen as entirely fictitious. And so it can happen that someone thinks he is innocently confiding in a friend or in his son, only to discover that in reality he has been speaking with a functionary serving the political regime, so that these relationships are suddenly to be interpreted as "official" and had even previously been such. Phenomena of this kind have meanwhile become an established part of experience in our time.

It has thus become clear enough where the rules of the game of an organization have their limits. The boundary is reached or transgressed where the rules are absolutized and thus leave no room for the personal freedom of the individual, or for relationships between persons in a community which cannot be subordinated to any set of rational aims.

V. Necessary overlap of rules of the game

Just as the individual person, in his concrete existence, combines in himself the three elements of the common, the individual and the personal, in the corresponding forms of human association all three elements appear in such a way that none of them has absolute dominance. Community, society and organization are such that, while none of them is simply reducible to any of the others, each affirms its particular form of commitment between people; and the different rules of the game appropriate to each of them never assume such an absolute importance that the others are completely irrelevant to them. This constitutes, so to speak, the "morality" of all that has been said up to this point. More precisely, two things are being said here: first, that the absolutizing of one of the three forms of association is in contradiction with true human reality; and second, that it is equally in contradiction with reality – even in those social structures which naturally and justifiably are characterized by the precedence they give to a particular form of association and the rules of the game appropriate to it – to attribute exclusive weight to this precedence.

I

The absolutizing of a particular form of association in contradiction with concrete human reality is not only theoretically wrong, it also leads, of necessity, to unfruitful and perhaps destructive target setting or confrontations. Thus it is false and at the same time futile to proclaim "community" as the ideal form of association. The family model cannot be the guideline for all human modes of associating. For example, the contractual balancing of interests can never follow the norms of community life. Absolutizing the community ideal will never rid us of the indeed reprehensible, uninhibited drive to assert one's own interests; it will be necessary for "society" to be seen and made plausible as a real possibility and likewise as a valid guideline for human collaboration in life. The direct opposite of injustice is not love but justice in which, oversimplifying somewhat, we have said the rules of the game of society can be summed up. But the "organization" mode also has its own independent and essential place in the life we share. It can be healthy and fruitful only if there is planned organization of "special" functions – as opposed to the common functions. This requires having both a hierarchy in the membership and distance of the management from the rest.

The overvaluing of the "social" form of association propagated by individualist liberalism is just as repugnant to reality as is the absolutizing of the community form. Basically it sees all human interaction – from family to state – as a network of contractual relationships between individuals. In its extreme form, which is unfortunately no longer altogether inconceivable, but also fortunately not completely achievable, such an absolutizing of "society" would not only lead to the dissolution of all community bonds – above all of the family – but also to the endangerment of the *bonum commune*, the common good as a whole, which demands the organization of all productive forces and can only be safeguarded where genuine political leadership is able to function effectively.

Absolutizing the "organization" is especially dangerous to our lives and is also of extremely current relevance. Its slogan is "total planning" and it aims at shaping social life along military lines, as can be seen from the favored terminology [work brigades]. What is more or less their declared aim, but is again, fortunately, one they cannot achieve, is the organization of the political body as an army of workers comprising nothing but individual functionaries who relate to one another primarily as co-workers. The inevitable but largely desired consequence is the destruction of the private sphere, the negation of personal freedom and the dissolution of all common life that is not reducible to the purely rational.

In contrast to all of this, social philosophy must remain aware of both the rights and limitations of all three forms of association.

II

Even in concrete social relationships in which one of the three fundamental forms predominates, this predominance is not to be absolutized, because otherwise the truly human spheres would be infringed upon. Even in the community and in an organization, the individual remains a personal being who exists for the sake of his own perfection and completion. And also in society people are still "brothers" even though they see themselves primarily as sovereign individuals and act as such.

It is true that in families and friendships, the rules of love, self-sacrifice, directness, and intimacy characterize relationships. However, even here, in a healthy situation

the individual's right to his personal sphere is still respected. This is where the rules of community run up
against their natural boundaries. A healthy and viable
family situation is then, at the same time, affected by social rules which, while perhaps subliminal, have practical
validity. And also the organizational aspect plays its part
– for example, in the division of responsibilities between
husband and wife in the running of the house and in the
education of children. One could even say that a family
that does not function in this way organizationally can
hardly be called a proper community.

A community in its ideal form will make room not
only for the characteristic predominant aspects of sharing
but also for the autonomy and private sphere of the individual: self-preservation along with self-sacrifice, advantage along with yielding. It will furthermore take into
account the "special" capabilities and leanings of its members and leave open to them, as they are integrated into
the life of the community, the possibility of a corresponding function. Such balance between the dominance of the
community aspect on the one hand and the social and organizational aspects on the other hand is, for example, the
way the Church differs from a sect, which is usually characterized by exaggeration of the communal element.

Also in the contractual balance of interests in the market place, in the social intercourse with unfamiliar persons
and, in general, in everyday dealings with the public in
our middle-class existences, it is natural that the "social"
rules of the game are predominant. But if the community's
rules were not somehow at the same time in force, "social"
co-existence, with its calculating meanness, would become completely inhuman. And the individualistic cult of
equality for which relationships of a purely "social" kind

are sometimes rightly blamed would lead to complete sterility if carried to the point of ignoring what is qualitatively special in individual persons. A social relationship of the primarily "social" kind will be most successful where, alongside the individuality of the members, what is common to them as well as what is particular to them is taken into account. Naturally, for example, the relationship between business partners does not function on the basis of friendship or shared labor in the whole venture but on the basis of advantage and profit for both parties. But if there is no trace of community in this relationship the business will finally suffer. And if both parties, according to the abilities and leanings "peculiar" to each of them, share the technical and commercial management of the business, the advantage will accrue to the individual persons which was the reason for the relationship being entered into in the first place.

The army and industrial businesses are, of course, first and foremost "organizations" which follow the rules of the game of an organization. However, no organization can last without the element of solidarity characteristic of the community. And it would destroy its own foundations if it were not to respect its co-workers' equal rights to human dignity and were completely to subordinate their personal freedom to the technical requirements involved in the performance of their function. A firm will not only be more human, but it will also work more fruitfully in the organizational sense, the less the purely functional element swallows up the element of community and the personal. A tank crew, for example, in which the right balance is struck between the community aspect of camaraderie and respect for the autonomy of the individual, while retaining the primacy of the organizational, could, from the sociological ["histological"] point of view, hardly be more ideal.

In our time, in which the rules of the game regarding performance of a function in sharing labor are inevitably becoming more important, it is clearly necessary to make sure of two things. First, the organizational form of association together with its particular characteristics of commitment and hierarchy has to be understood clearly as a genuine human possibility. On the other hand, given the new age of comprehensive planning, it is vital consciously to reinforce and cultivate the natural dams of resistance against the dangers of absolutizing organization. These dams are the sense of community, above all of family, and respect for personal dignity and human freedom.

VI. The Masses, struggle and power, unplanned "organization"

The Masses

The term "masses" is used in normal speech and thought, even in the sociological and scientific context, with widely differing meanings. Sometimes it means a relatively large gathering of people. It is used like this in Gustave le Bon's well-known book "Psychologie der Masse" which appeared in 1895 and which, like Ferdinand Toennies's book, achieved a certain classical status but is quite lacking in clarity with regard to its fundamental concepts. Sigmund Freud[32] follows Le Bon's rather vague terminology and refers to every somewhat extensive social grouping as "Masse" – even the Church and the army. Sometimes the word has been used with perjorative overtones [lower class, *plebs*, *vulgus*] which then seemed to provoke the reaction of giving the term an entirely positive value in stressing the revolutionary role of the proletariat.

In contrast to all of this, but at the same time claiming to be just as much in line with human language as it is really spoken, the term "masses" is used as a clearly distinguishable basic human form of social relationship, though, of course, not as a basic form of association in the strict

32 Massenpsychologie und Ich-Analyse

sense. Real association, as I hope I have made clear, is based on a mutually affirmed bond; and precisely this is what is missing in the crowd, although on the other hand exactly what is common to the individuals is the visually striking element. This is again the reason why the crowd, looked at superficially, seems to be a conspiratorial community and can be mistaken for one. It has rightly been said[33] that the crowd is a social grouping "in which each individual participates only with that part of his personality which he has in common with others and which then comes to the forefront." And whenever, for example, the excitement of a violently demonstrating crowd reaches its boiling point; when in the arena or the stadium enthusiasm for the bullfighter or for the hero in a sporting contest breaks out in loud roars of applause; when a political sect is intoxicated by the rallying cry of the demagogue – always when a large group of people become a crowd, the distinctions in individuals' ways of life, character, intelligence and calling immediately disappear; that which distinguishes between them becomes, in fact, unimportant and is lost; each one behaves like all the others; what marks the individual as a distinct person is absorbed into the undifferentiated crowd in their mass activity. The individual who loses himself in this way, however much he may insist on his own personal "distinction," becomes less and less concerned with who it is beside him who waves his arms, shouts , or pats him on the shoulder. The foreground, even of his consciousness, is at least for a time taken up with one opinion, mode of expression, and action.

However, the crowd is not a unit and it does not have a group identity. It is a plurality made up of individuals

33 See W. Vlengels, Die Masse

who basically "mean nothing to one another." They are not only not bound to one another in mutual affirmation: in truth, each of them remains "just himself." This is precisely what distinguishes the crowd from the community: in the latter the communal quality is achieved and lasts because of the inwardly free dispensing with self-assertion. In the crowd, on the other hand, what the individuals have in common is not a result of self-sacrifice but of an external force which overruns, enraptures, and blots out the self.

The transitory aspect of the relationships – intrinsic to the nature of crowds – is proof that a more profound bond never existed. The individuals who, without inhibition, had just been ecstatically giving vent to their convictions and desires, part company without noticing any dissolution of the bond and without any greeting or saying goodbye. They no longer know one another.

One could call the behavior characteristic of crowds "participation." And it is participation for the sake of participation without any insight into an objective need and without any declared bond between the individuals.

Just how problematic the "common element" is within the crowd at a massed gathering can be seen with special clarity in the highly characteristic and, at the same time, somewhat paradoxical phenomenon of *panic*. It is paradoxical insofar as where there is panic the equality stance borders directly on the relationship of power. Each individual tries to assert himself at the expense of all the others. For this reason panic has been seen as a characteristic form of expression of crowds – as both their "negation"[34] and "disintegration" [Freud]. If a fire breaks out in a

34 See E. Gothein, Soziologie der Panik

theatre all follow the same impulse; but each one, without consideration for his neighbor, who is possibly trampled down, seeks, with all the might at his disposal, to save himself.

Relationship between conflict and violence

As with society as a form of association, the human relationship characterized by conflict and power is crystallized in the individuality of the partners. Here, too, we have to do with a real social relationship insofar as there can be no conflict "without one another"; but unlike the case of "society," this is not a form of association, which by definition is based on a mutually-affirmed bond. Thus, whereas in the "social" contractual relationship the "I and you" remains, in the conflict and power relationship there is simply an "I or you." In "society" self-assertion of the individual is limited and tempered by means of the mutual affirmation, but here it appears in an unmitigated form.

It is still necessary to distinguish between conflict and naked violence – quite apart from the fact that there is an element of "game" in conflicts. But even here there is an "I or you." A married couple playing chess with one another naturally strive, despite their untroubled relationship, for their own victory and the defeat of the other; as long as the game is in progress the rules of behavior pertaining to "community" are suspended. Friends who otherwise have "no secrets from one another" do not reveal anything about the cards they hold. Similarly, the differences in rank in an organization are of no significance in a contest; the partners are, for example, not primarily "boss" and "worker," but are individuals of equal standing who try, with all fair means, to knock out their opponent.

Here we must distinguish between two possible ways in which the norms of behavior can be violated. The first is when the conflict element of the contest only *seems* to be in force, whereas it is in fact omitted – for example, when Lieutenant Lucien Leuwen, the main character in Stendhal's unfinished novel, in a game of dominos with his military superior, "is wise enough to lose six games in a row." It can also happen that the "play" character of the context is spoilt by cheating or unfairness. This approximates to violence.

But in between there are several further forms of conflict which, while they can hardly be seen as "games," are still subject to norms which are binding and are to be accepted by the opposing sides. This applies not only to duels, in which it can in fact be a question of life and death, but also to today's sporting contests, in which, for example, a highly remunerative *Grand Prix* can be won, and in which the element of play has long since been lost. But in these cases there is a strict norm of behavior. This applies likewise even to the sport of boxing, which is distinguishable from the ancient Roman contest between gladiators: despite all the brutality, it is still not simply uninhibited violence. Thus the intelligent caricaturist's witty caption is more profoundly true than it might seem at first sight: "The boxing match cannot take place because the opponents have become enemies."

In relationships between individuals, the extreme case of violence in which the declared aim is to destroy the other person is only seldom realised. Yet it is possible, for example in rivalry in one's career or about a woman, for an enmity to exist – even one which is concealed, undeclared, perhaps existing under the guise of friend-ship – which aims unmercifully at the elimination of the other person. The plank of Carneades, so often cited in ca-suistics, has manifold applications. The famous ancient skeptic, Carneades, referred to the plank to which two shipwrecked people were clinging but which could only support one person. Here, not only does the norm of love – except in the case of heroic self-sacrifice – cease to have effect, but so does the norm of justice; and what remains is naked, ruthless self-assertion.

The violent acts of repression and destruction of de-fenceless minorities in areas controlled by totalitarian regimes not only lie outside the limits of the concept of "conflict"; they are even in no way to be seen as a "social relationship." Here there is no question of partnership or opposition. There is only a subject-object relationship. And the resistance fighter who, for example, standing in for others, undertakes to put his own self on the line against those in power and to challenge them under the motto "you or me," is thereby declaring himself ready for martyrdom.

In the political relationship between nations and power blocks, war which is aimed at the destruction of the enemy and is clearly carried out in the spirit of "you or me" seems to be an inevitable phenomenon – unless [hopefully] the destructive force of weapons reaches such a level that attempts at self-assertion through war are nec-essarily linked with the certainty of self-destruction.

Unplanned "organization"

Real organization depends on forward planning which unites individuals, according both to their particular gifts and bent, and to the particular function envisaged for them. However, even without such forward planning, co-operation can come about which serves a unified end and also – in an analogous, broad sense – can seem "organized" and can justifiably be referred to as such. In fact, even in literature[35] on the subject there has been reference to "spontaneous organization" and "unconscious division of functions." But naturally we are not speaking here either of a form of association or of actual rules of the game, although sometimes it might appear as if we were. In the time of the former *Wandervogel* youth movement, on journeys undertaken with three or four comrades, it happened mostly of itself that the same person would always look after the meals, another would look after the fire, and a third would put up the tent – and so forth. This was clearly collaboration, with separate functions, to achieve an end that was important to us all. And yet there was no fixed plan and no planner assigning the individual his task. Sometimes it was only afterwards that we realized which function each of us had spontaneously taken on. We were very good friends with one another and the natural, mutually affirmed bond was crystallized in what we had in common and not at all in the particularity of the functions each of us performed. The same kind of thing may well have been true, and may still be true on occasions, in small social groups. But this is not representative of current social reality in general.

For example, no one has expressly determined that in a village or in the suburb of a city there should be no more or no fewer grocery stores, chemist shops, bakery shops [etc.] than the population need; and for a time it may seem

35 R. Erdmann, Grundlagen einer Organisationslehre

as though this implied a spontaneous, unplanned "organization." Suddenly, however, unavoidable problems will arise, serious problems in which the lack of planning is faced with its limitations. The "free play of market forces" is, as then becomes clear, no longer adequate as sole regulator. Large concerns appear with their chain stores; there are bankruptcies and legal restrictions.

Also the free choice of profession, an achievement of middle-class society which, of course, certain social strata are still to a large extent unable to attain, has in the meantime, as everyone knows, become questionable. It seemed to guarantee an effective, though unplanned realization of what was necessary for the common good, but then, for example, a person convinced that he has the ability and calling to be a doctor finds that the *numerus clausus* excludes him from studying medicine. Perhaps he will also be told one day that there are enough doctors, and that engineers and experts in information technology are needed.

In a word: on the distant horizon, but not at all unannounced, there is the danger of a totalitarian organization of all social life. It is emerging in the worldwide historical process of division of labor. The end result could be a world army of labor – which would be seen by some as a terrifying eschatological vision and greeted by others as the realization of "concrete utopia."

Epilogue

This volume is a completely new formulation and a much shorter version of a book written in 1931 and published under the same title in 1933 [Herder Verlag, Freiburg]. After a review published at the time in Switzerland by a friend referred to it as "latently anti-totalitarian" the National Socialist regime forbade a second edition. After 1945 four slightly revised editions were published [in the Josef Knecht Verlag, Frankfurt] and another three in Dutch translation [Verlag Het Spectrum, Utrecht-Antwerp].

For the fundamental idea of the work – above all, the division into community-society-organization – I am indebted to the sociologist Johann Plenge, who was teaching at the University of Münster and at whose Research Institute for Organization Theory and Sociology I worked as Assistant from 1928 until 1932. Strangely, in various commentaries of his own, Plenge made his conceptual starting point almost unrecognizable as a result of unhelpful and misleading analogies. In the first version of this book I dealt with this in some detail. Furthermore, the arbitrary terminology of Plenge's theory of "more" (Mehrschaftslehre) has not been used in this current version.

Anyone who is interested in a critical report on the sociological literature on the theme of "Basic forms of association" (Grundformen der Gesellung) [W. Sombart, L. v. Wiese, Th. Geiger et al.] might consult the notes in earlier editions, in which, above all, there is a lengthy essay analysing the work of Ferdinand Toennies.

It was, in the broadest sense, a social and pedagogical impulse which led to the decision to make available a new version of that early book which had been out of print for twenty years. I was concerned that the widely- voiced demand for education about living together should be freed from primitive oversimplifications ["Changing society into a community"] and based on the more differentiated insight that there are several legitimate fundamental forms of living together and therefore different ways of being "just" to one's fellow men – by understanding and putting into practise the rules of the game of community, society and organization as meaningful norms of behavior.

Bibliography

In the following literature overview, works written in the period after the Second World War are few in number. The reason for this fact, which at first sight perhaps seems odd, is that, unlike in the period prior to 1933, the theme dealt with in this new work [as a review in the magazine "Soziale Welt," 1967, observed with critical regret], "the system of rules of the game is no longer the subject of sociological inquiry."

Aelred von Rieval, Die heilige Freundschaft. Munich n.d.

A. *Bogdanow*, Allgemeine Organiationslehre, 2 vols. Berlin 1926/28

G. *le Bon*, Psychologie der Massen. 4th edition, Stuttgart 1922

G. *Briefs*, Sozialform und Sozialgeist der Gegenwart, in: Handwörterbuch der Soziologie

J. *Cambon*, Le diplomate. Paris 1926

L. *Clausen/F. U. Pappi* [eds], Ankunft bei Toennies. Soziologische Beiträge zum 125. Geburtstag von F. Toennies. Kiel 1981

G. *Colm*, Masse, in: Handwörterbuch der Soziologie

F. *Delekat*, Was ist und wie entsteht Gemeinschaft?, in: F. Krueger, Philosophie der Gemeinschaft. Berlin 1929

K. *Dunkmann*, Die Bedeutung der Kategorien Gemeinschaft und Gesellschaft für die Geisteswissenschaft, in: Kölner Vierteljahreshefte für Soziologie, No. 5

F. *Eberstein*, Die Organisation bei Karl Marx. Essen 1921

R. *Erdmann*, Grundlagen einer Organisationslehre. Leipzig 1921

Th. *Erismann*, Der Massenmensch, in: Jahrbuch für Charakterologie IV. Berlin 1927

S. *Freud*, Massenpsychologie und Ich-Analyse. Leipzig 1923

H. *Freyer*, Einleitung in die Soziologie. Leipzig, 1931

—Gemeinschaft und Volk, in: F. Krueger, Philosophie der Gemeinschaft. Berlin 1929

—Soziologie als Wirklichkeitswissenschaft. Leipzig 1930

Th. *Geiger*, Die Gestalten der Gesellung. Karlsruhe 1928

—Die Gruppe und die Kategorien Gemeinschaft und Gesellschaft, in: Archiv für Sozialwissenschaft und Sozialpolitik. Vol. 58

—Die Masse und ihre Aktion. Stuttgart 1926

—Gemeinschaft, in: Handwörterbuch der Soziologie

—Gesellschaft, in: Handwörterbuch der Soziologie

E. *Gothein*, Soziologie der Panik, in: Verhandlungen des 1. Deutschen Soziologentages. Tübingen 1911

R. *Guardini*, Möglichkeiten und Grenzen der Gemeinschaft, in: Die Musikpflege. 1930

Handwörterbuch der Soziologie. Stuttgart 1931; reprinted Stuttgart 1959

D. *v. Hildebrand*, Metaphysik der Gemeinschaft. Munich 1930

S. Kracauer, Die Angestellten. Frankfurt 1930

E. Lohmeyer, Vom Begriff der religiösen Gemeinschaft. Leipzig 1925

Cl. Münster, Mengen, Massen, Kollektive. Munich 1952

F. Oppenheimer, System der Soziologie I. Jena 1922/23

B. Pieper, Familie im Urteil ihrer Therapeuten. Bausteine einer Theorie familialer Arbeit. Frankfurt-New York 1986

J. Pieper, Die Grundbegriffe L. v. Wieses, in: Kölner Vierteljahreshefte für Soziologie. No. 9

—"Wirklichkeitswissenschaftliche" Soziologie, in: Archiv für Sozialwissenschaft und Sozialpolitik. Vol. 66

—Über die Spannung zwischen Organisation und Gemeinschaft in der kirchlichen Arbeit, in: Magazin für Pädagogik. 97 [1934]

—Das Gesellungsideal der industriellen Arbeitswelt. Aufriß einer sozialpädagogischen Grundfrage, in: Pharus. 23 [1934]

—Über soziale Ideale und Fehlideale, in: Bildung und Erziehung. 1936

J. Plenge, Das Problemsystem der theoretischen Soziologie, in: Kölner Vierteljahreshefte für Soziologie. No. 8

—Drei Vorlesungen über die allgemeine Organisationslehre. Essen 1919

—Acht Glossen zum Betrieb der Gesellschaftslehre, in: Kölner Vierteljahreshefte für Soziologie. No. 9

H. Plessner, Grenzen der Gemeinschaft. Bonn 1924

B. Schäfers, Soziologie des Jugendalters. Leverkusen 1982

—Gemeinschaft und Gesellschaft. Zur Entwicklung und Aktualität eines Begriffpaares, in: Gesellschaft, Staat, Erziehung. No 32 1983

Bibliography

A. Schäffle, Bau und Leben des sozialen Körpers. 2nd edition. Tübingen 1896

L. L. Schücking, Die Familie im Puritanismus. Leipzig 1929

G. Schwägler, Soziologie der Familie. Ursprung und Entwicklung. Tübingen 1970

M. zu Solms, Bau und Gliederung der Menschengruppen. Karlsruhe 1929

W. Sombart, Die Grundformen des menschlichen Zusammenlebens, in: Handwörterbuch der Soziologie

L. v. Stein, Der Begriff der Gesellschaft und die soziale Geschichte der Französischen Revolution bis 1830. Leipzig 1850

F. Toennies, Gemeinschaft und Gesellschaft. 6/7 edition. Berlin 1926. Reprint of 8th edition Darmstadt 1979

— Gemeinschaft und Gesellschaft, in: Handwörterbuch der Soziologie

—Selbstdarstellung, in: Philosophie in Selbstdarstellung. Leipzig 1922

—Soziologische Studien und Kritiken. I, II. Jena 1925/26[*]

W. Vershofen, Die Stufen zur Sozietät. Nürnberg 1931

A. Vierkandt, Gesellschaftslehre. Stuttgart 1928

W. Vleugels, Die Masse. Munich 1930

---

[*] There is a review of the first edition of this book. It was written in 1935 but [for political reasons] remained unpublished. It is housed, together with correspondence about it, as a manuscript in the "Ferdinand-Toennies-Archiv" of the Schleswig-Holstein State Library in Kiel.

To celebrate the centenary of F. Toennies's birth, several articles appeared in the Kölner Zeitschrift für Soziologie und Sozialpsychologie. 7 [1955].

G. *Walther*, Ein Beitrag zur Ontologie der sozialen Gemeinschaften. Halle 1923

L. *v. Wiese*, Allgemeine Soziologie. 2 vols. Munich 1924/29

—Beziehungssoziologie, in: Handwörterbuch der Soziologie

—Systematische Soziologie in Deutschland, in: Kölner Vierteljahreshefte für Soziologie. No. 8

—Randbemerkungen zu Dr. Piepers Kritik, in: Kölner Vierteljahreshefte für Soziologie. No. 9

Index of Names